WESTON-SUPER-MARE
THEN & NOW
IN COLOUR

SHARON POOLE

The
History
Press

First published in 2012

The History Press
The Mill, Brimscombe Port
Stroud, Gloucestershire, GL5 2QG
www.thehistorypress.co.uk

British Library Cataloguing in Publication Data.
A catalogue record for this book is available from the British Library.

ISBN 978 0 7524 6795 5

Typesetting and origination by The History Press
Manufacturing managed by Jellyfish Print Solutions Ltd
Printed in India.

CONTENTS

ACKNOWLEDGEMENTS

My thanks must go to the many people who have lent me photographs over the years and without whom this book would not be possible; in particular I would like to thank Gwen Ellis, Revd Peter Gregory, Mary Macfarlane, Andrew Palmer, Denis Salisbury, Michael Tozer, the late Edward Amesbury and the late Ena Howe.

ABOUT THE AUTHOR

Sharon Poole moved to Weston in 1971, the same year she began to work for the Museum Service. Part of her work at this time involved compiling a photographic record of Weston and the many changes that were occurring during this period. Over the subsequent years Sharon became curator of the local and social history collections at North Somerset Museum. Her first book was published in 1987 and since then she has written many more on Weston and the surrounding area. She left the Museum Service in 2001 but continues to take an active interest in the history of Weston and currently works as a freelance speaker, writer and researcher.

INTRODUCTION

I sometimes wonder what an occupant of Village Weston would think if he or she could see Weston-super-Mare today. The boundary of their village ended around what is now Alfred Street to the east and Locking Road to the south. Nowadays the urban sprawl reaches out into the once green fields of Worle, St Georges and Locking, and completely encompasses the one-time hamlet of Milton. Uphill alone has survived more or less intact, protected by its geography, which creates a natural boundary around the settlement.

The origins of Weston-super-Mare go back many thousands of years. People settled here in the Bronze Age, and on the crown of Worlebury there is an Iron Age hillfort, built over 2,000 years ago. This came to a violent end, from evidence of burnt walls and skeletons found with sword cuts on their limbs and skulls. In Norman times a church was built in the village. This was on the same site as the current parish church in Lower Church Road, which replaced it in 1827. From medieval times until the seventeenth century the village changed little, with fishing and farming the main occupations. In the late eighteenth century doctors 'discovered' the seaside, leading people to abandon the inland spas as coastal resorts began to develop. At the time of the first census in 1801 the population was 128. Just twenty-one years later, when the first visitor's guide was published, there were 738 people. From then on, the pace of development rarely slackened, spurred on by the arrival of a branch of Brunel's Bristol & Exeter Railway in 1841. The village became a town the following year, with the passing of an Improvement Act, and by the end of the nineteenth century, there were 20,000 residents. The population of Weston-super-Mare currently stands at almost 83,000.

Change is natural and continual, and often barely noticed, but in just the last few years there have been some major alterations to the landscape around us – the most dramatic being the fire that destroyed the Grand Pier pavilion. Other losses include the Royal Pier Hotel (again to fire), Overcombe in the Shrubbery and the Bayside Hotel, once Devonshire Cottage and better-known as the Cairo Hotel, at the bottom of Highbury Road.

Conversely, the pier has been rebuilt with a new landmark pavilion, and there has been major regeneration of the seafront with a newly surfaced and widened promenade and interesting sculptural features. At the same time it has created improved flood defences and protection should sea levels rise over the coming years. Princess Royal Square has also been redesigned and largely pedestrianised. With the cast-iron Coalbrookdale fountain restored as its centrepiece and placed in a new setting with extensive seating, flower beds and lawns, the seafront has a new focus for enjoying warm summer evenings.

It is probably enough to let the images speak for themselves. I find the comparisons fascinating, if not always favourable, but that is a personal opinion. I hope you enjoy browsing through these photographs, finding out how the town used to look, what has changed and, in a few cases, how little has changed. As to what the future holds for the town – we will have to wait to discover.

Sharon Poole, September 2011

ANCHOR HEAD

ANCHOR HEAD AND Birnbeck Pier, 1905 (right). This interesting photograph shows the southern steamer jetty on Birnbeck Pier being rebuilt after it had been wrecked in what became known as the Great Gale in September 1903. Progress was slow and it did not reopen for another four years. On the pier itself you can see the switchback railway. The buildings on the right are part of the Royal Pier Hotel. It was built in 1854 as a hotel but until 1870 was Anchor Head School under the supervision of Dr Godfrey. You can still see traces of a swimming pool for the use of the pupils cut in the rocks below.

BIRNBECK PIER FROM Anchor Head, 2011. The southern jetty in the picture above was dismantled in 1923 so that a concrete platform could be built to increase the surface area of the island. The Royal Pier Hotel has gone completely now. A series of fires, the worst being in September 2010, resulted in the

remains having to be demolished. Plans have recently been submitted to develop the area with a seven-storey apartment complex with shops and cafés at the promenade level. Anchor Head is a popular sheltered cove for sunbathers and children exploring rock pools. In the early nineteenth century it used to be the ladies' bathing place. The concrete slipway in the foreground was used to board pleasure boats in the early years of the twentieth century.

BIRNBECK PIER

BIRNBECK PIER WITH a White Funnel Fleet steamer at the northern jetty, *c.*1904 (below).
Birnbeck Pier, which opened in 1867, is unique in that it links an island to the mainland. Both the
original jetties were badly damaged in the great storm that hit the town in 1903. The northern
jetty (on the right) was originally made of wood but after the gale it was rebuilt in steel, 50ft
longer and 5ft wider than the previous one. The southern jetty (on the left) took longer to rebuild
and it is still in a wrecked condition in this photograph. It reopened in 1909 but was dismantled
permanently in 1923 so that a large concrete platform could be built on the island to increase the
land area. Among the cluster of buildings you can see the clock tower to the right, a bandstand just
left of the tower and the undulating track of the switchback railway on the left of that.

BIRNBECK PIER, SEPTEMBER 2011. Today the Grade II* listed structure is derelict. A succession of new owners have come up with ideas on how to restore and revive the pier but as yet nothing has been done. The pier was sold again in September 2011 to the same company that plans to redevelop the Royal Pier Hotel site and we can but wait and see what transpires. On the island, the clock tower is still standing, along with a few of the old buildings. In the centre is the new steel lifeboat house. In 2008 the RNLI stopped using the 1902 lifeboat house and slipway (the longest in the country at almost 113m) and changed to tractor and carriage launching, which offers greater flexibility, especially at low tide.

PRINCE CONSORT GARDENS

PRINCE CONSORT GARDENS and Birkett Road, from the approach road to Birnbeck Pier, *c.*1903 (right). This part of Weston was originally known as Flagstaff Hill. It was laid out as public gardens in the mid 1860s by the Smyth-Pigott family, who owned the land. As the family's fortunes waned towards the end of the nineteenth century, Cecil Smyth-Pigott offered the gardens to the town. These terraces were constructed to provide walks and seating areas and to discourage noisy games that might devalue neighbouring properties!

The excavated stone was used in the building of the seafront promenade. The timber and glass shelter was built in 1900 and bears an elaborate date stone in the centre gable.

PRINCE CONSORT GARDENS and Kewstoke Road, 2011. The foreground railings have gone, probably for salvage during the Second World War. The shrubs have grown considerably and there is a 1970s block of flats to the left of Rockwood. The shelter remains unaltered though, allowing uninterrupted views across Birnbeck Pier to Wales. The two large Victorian villas were once part of Westcliffe School and later, Weston College. In recent years they have been sympathetically converted into apartments. While the pier remains derelict and with the loss of the Royal Pier Hotel, this area has become a car park.

GLENTWORTH BAY

PRINT OF GLENTWORTH Bay and Birnbeck Road, *c*.1855 (below). The little castle-like building on the rocks was the bathing house that belonged to Claremont Lodge, which is the three-gabled house to the left of the Royal Pier Hotel. This print shows just how grand the early seafront mansions were, with their landscaped gardens and sea views. On the hilltop the stone walls of the Iron Age hillfort of Worlebury can be seen. The woods were only some thirty years old at this time and had not grown to mask this important archaeological site. It was about this date that the site was first fully excavated, the finds including human skeletons, charred grain and animal bones. This picture also shows the

natural beach. The promenade was not built until the 1880s and the Marine Lake some forty years after that. Until then this was the centuries-old rocky shoreline known to local fishermen.

GLENTWORTH BAY, AUGUST 2011. Aside from the development of Claremont, the greatest change from the earlier view is the building of the promenade. This huge project was begun in 1883 but not extended as far as Birnbeck until three years later. In 1927 Marine Lake was built to create an area of beach with water available for paddling etc. at all states of the tide. Nowadays the rowing boats are back on the lake, together with more contemporary amusements. The large villas lining Birnbeck Road are now hotels or nursing homes. The tree growth on the top of Worlebury totally hides the hillfort from view.

BIRNBECK ROAD

BIRNBECK ROAD FROM Glentworth Bay, *c.*1901 (below). The villas pictured are, from the left: Grosvenor Villas, Rozel Villas, Elizabethan Villas (with the two gables), Corfield House, Sutherland House and Beaufort Villas. These mansions were large even for when they were built and most were soon used as boarding houses and hotels. The left part of the promenade in this photograph was known as Madeira Cove and had a small stage for band recitals and concert parties. Again, you can see the natural shingle beach.

MADEIRA COVE, 2011. Most of the old villas are still recognisable, even with the modern ground-floor extensions. The exception is the new block of forty-eight apartments that replaced the Rozel Hotel and Marlborough Holiday Flats in 2004. The Rozel Hotel closed in November 2001 after being run for some eighty years by the Chapman family. The name Rozel came from Rozel Bay in Jersey, where Albert Bodman, founder of the hotel and great-grandfather of the last owner, Tony Chapman, stayed for his honeymoon. On the promenade is No. 2 in a series of six wooden sculptures entitled 'Light & Shadow' by Michael Fairfax. The top of this sculpture echoes the shape of Brean Down in the distance, while the vertical wave pattern was taken from the balconies of the buildings behind.

THE ROZEL BANDSTAND

ROZEL BANDSTAND, 1950s (right). This area has undergone many changes over the years. In 1920 a small semi-circular bandstand was built here, known as the Dutch Oven because of its shape. This sheltered the orchestra, but the audience and conductor were left out in the open air – not so good in the rain! In 1935 the first Rozel Bandstand was built, with some covered seating at the back. This was made possible by extending the promenade out over the beach, with a colonnade running underneath. In 1937 the bandstand was completely rebuilt as in this picture, with a windscreen for the audience, raised seating at the back and a café. The stage was in the square building in the centre of this photograph.

MADEIRA COVE, 2011. The building in the centre is all that remains of the old Rozel Bandstand. On 13 December 1981 a severe gale wrecked much of the promenade, including the colonnade at Marine Lake. The damage was so severe it had to be demolished and with it the Rozel Bandstand. What was left was rebuilt as a restaurant. The white building left of centre is Claremont Wine Vaults, built in 1850, originally as shops but soon becoming a pub. Rozel House on the right is an apartment block built in 2004 on the site of two Victorian villas.

MANILLA CRESCENT AND GLENTWORTH HALL

MANILLA CRESCENT AND Glentworth Hall, *c.*1903 (right). Manilla Crescent was built in 1851, and Glentworth Hall, on the right, was built two years later for the Cox family. It later became Hazelhurst School (with tennis courts behind) before being converted into a hotel in 1926. Behind Manilla Crescent you can just see the tower of Holy Trinity church. On the promenade a few people are walking and there are two smart carriages in the road. Just to the left of the central lamp post is a horse drinking-trough.

MANILLA CRESCENT AND Glentworth Court, August 2011. The different paint colours and the
various alterations to the roofline over the years have left this crescent unrecognisable as such.
Glentworth Hall was demolished in 1973. A few years previously, planning permission had been
granted to replace the building with flats and Weston's first motel but this scheme never came to
fruition. It was developed with this apartment block on the site of the hotel, while behind it, on the
old tennis courts is now Madeira Court – a block of sixty-seven sheltered flats for the over sixties.
In the background Holy Trinity church is now the Elim Pentecostal church. The promenade now
has a wall on both sides, built as part of the new flood defence system completed in 2011.

KNIGHTSTONE &
MARINE LAKE

ROUGH SEAS AT Glentworth Bay, photographed by Ethel Hopwood, *c.*1908 (left). Before Marine Lake was created this was a popular part of the seafront to watch the waves crashing against the sea wall. Beyond Knightstone causeway there is a forest of masts from the boats in the harbour. These would have been mostly colliers bringing coal over from Wales for the gas works and Royal Pottery, while in the background is the Grand Pier pavilion and further in the distance, Uphill Old church.

KNIGHTSTONE AND THE Grand Pier from Marine Lake, August 2011. The seas no longer batter the promenade here, since Marine Lake was built in 1927. The buildings on Knightstone, including the theatre, swimming pool and Dr Fox's Bathhouse, have all been converted into residential properties together with a couple of cafés. Additional apartment blocks were built between the original buildings but there is still public access around the island and across Marine Lake causeway, with a new sloping ramp for wheelchair users who were previously prevented from crossing the causeway by the steep flight of steps at the Knightstone end. The new complex was officially opened by HM the Queen in July 2007.

KNIGHTSTONE ROAD

ALBERT BUILDINGS, KNIGHTSTONE Road, c.1900 (right). Built in 1843, this is the middle of the three terraces along Knightstone Road. The cast-iron street furniture is striking and the broad sweep of the empty promenade indicates that this picture was taken in the winter. In the road there is a horse-drawn carriage with two occupants and in front, a man pushing a hand barrow. Just in front of the barrow, one of the properties has an amazing arched gateway in topiary. The properties were all private homes or boarding houses at this date.

ALBERT BUILDINGS, AUGUST 2011. This terrace has changed almost beyond recognition. The properties are all now hotels and bars. An extra storey has been added to every building and the ground floors have been extended out to the front to create additional bar space with balconies at first-floor level. The road is now narrower, since the promenade was widened as part of the new flood prevention scheme, completed in 2011. The new wall on the road side of the promenade is intended to trap any water that is washed over the sea wall and entrances are protected by flood gates which are closed when bad weather is forecast. Interest is provided by the polished granite seating and huge chunks of local limestone.

KNIGHTSTONE ROAD DRINKING FOUNTAIN

THE DRINKING FOUNTAIN, Knightstone Road, *c.*1900 (below). Behind the fountain is the thatched Whitecross Dairy. This was built in 1791 as a holiday cottage for the Revd W. Leeves of Wrington. In the centre are the backs of Royal Crescent while on the right are Beachfield Villas, built in 1841 by Thomas Harrill on the site of Sheppard's farmhouse. At the time they were

thought to be much too grand for Weston and the rector told Mr Harrill that he would never find anyone with the means to live in them! One of those who did have the means in 1842 was Thomas Smith, one the first town commissioners and a great public servant to Weston. In the right foreground is another of the drinking troughs for the many horses that pulled wagonettes, carriages and carts up and down the seafront.

THE OLD THATCHED Cottage Restaurant, August 2011. This is the second oldest building surviving in Weston after Glebe House and the only one to retain a thatched roof. When the Weston-super-Mare Improvement and Market Act of 1842 was passed, all new properties had to have a tiled roof as thatch was a fire hazard as well as impossible to fit gutters to, so pedestrians were liable to get very wet on occasion. Beachfield Villas have been extended and are now part of the Lauriston Hotel, a specially adapted hotel for the visually-impaired. The public drinking fountain and horse trough are long gone and the promenade widened, re-surfaced and a wall built along the road side as part of the new flood prevention scheme completed in 2011.

ROYAL TERRACE

ROYAL TERRACE FROM the Promenade, *c.*1890 (below). This elegant building, which has turrets at each end, was built in the 1860s. This is the back of the terrace, with the main entrances along Knightstone Road. The Royal Hotel can just be glimpsed behind the bushes. The foundation stone for

the hotel was laid about 1807. The builder was Charles Taylor of Milton, and he later became the first manager. The hotel's fortunes fluctuated wildly over the first few years but it survived and is still welcoming guests today. The couple in the carriage look well-to-do, with their own vehicle and driver. The gentleman is wearing a top hat and the lady is sheltering under an umbrella, as is the lady pedestrian behind them.

ROYAL TERRACE, 2011. The building is largely unaltered although, once again, the different paint colours have spoiled the symmetry of the terrace. The shrubs surrounding what was once the sunken tennis court for the Royal Hotel have gone. The Cabot, on the left, was converted from an elegant Regency villa, known as Esplanade Cottage, and a seafront house built in the 1850s. In the foreground is one of the new seats built into the flood defence wall of the promenade.

GRAND PIER

ON THE GRAND Pier, late 1920s (above). This picture was taken between 1927, when the central shelter with seating was built, and 1930 when the Edwardian pavilion was destroyed by fire. The pavilion housed a beautiful theatre that could seat 2,000, with another 300 standing around the upper balcony. The interior was very ornate: for example, the ceiling was divided into nine panels painted with sky scenes and each edged with pink and gilded embellishments. When the pier opened in 1904, the *Weston Gazette* newspaper reported that it was 'lit at over 250 points with 500 incandescent electric lamps of varying power.' Productions included opera, musical comedy, music hall, Shakespeare, ballet and boxing. Among the famous stars that trod its boards were Anna Pavlova, George Robey, Vesta Tilley, Sir Ralph Richardson, Mrs Patrick Campbell, Dame Clara Butt, Jack Hulbert and Cicely Courtneidge. Outside, at first-floor level, there was a balcony on which visitors could stroll, admire the views or simply listen to the band in the bandstand in front of the pavilion.

ON THE GRAND Pier, 2011. A view of the third pavilion on this pier, opened in 2010. After the theatre burnt down in 1930, the replacement pavilion became an amusement hall, the largest on any pier in Britain. In 2008 that art deco structure was also lost in a huge fire, visible even in Wales across the Bristol Channel. As in 1930, a new larger building was planned as a replacement. Local residents chose their favourite design from among several options put forward and the Grand Pier is now a popular all-year-round attraction, with conference areas and even a wedding venue. Although the 1920s cast-iron wind screen down the centre survived the 2008 fire, it was removed and replaced with a double-sided screen with opening panels, so that in wet or windy weather, people can walk to the pavilion and still keep dry.

THE SANDS

CHILDREN PADDLING ON the sands, *c.*1904 (below). Behind the children is the then recently opened Grand Pier and pavilion. The boats are flatners, used as fishing boats throughout the winter and as pleasure boats during the summer months. Their flat bottom meant they stayed upright when the tide went out and the shallow draft enabled them to sail close to the nets to collect the fish on an ebbing tide. Before Birnbeck Pier was built in 1867, a 'gull-yeller' was

Grand Pier Pavilion Westo.

employed at the Birnbeck fishery to shout
and scare the birds away until the fishermen
got there to gather in the catch.

GRAND PIER AND sands, September 2011.
A lovely view of a magnificent pier.
At high tide it achieved perfectly that
sensation of being on a ship at sea but
with no risk of feeling sick. On the sands a
group of donkeys have just been unloaded
from their transport vehicle ready to carry
children up and down the beach for the day.
Donkeys have been on Weston Beach for
hundreds of years. They were first used by
fishermen to carry the catch or cart seaweed
from the beach to the fields as fertiliser.
When the first visitors arrived in the early
nineteenth century, they would hire a donkey
and ride out to explore neighbouring villages.
By the mid nineteenth century they were
giving rides on the beach and pulling donkey
wheelchairs around the town.

ROGERS' FIELD AND THE WINTER GARDENS

ROYAL TERRACE AND the Royal Hotel from the Grand Pier, 1904 (below). Taken from the first-floor balcony on the Grand Pier pavilion, you can see the open green spaces of Grove Park to the left and Rogers' Field to the right. The field got its name from the one-time owner of the Royal Hotel, Thomas Rogers, to which it belonged and which still holds covenants over the land, restricting the height of any developments to protect their views. The hotel used it to graze their own cows which provided milk for guests.

ROYAL TERRACE AND the Winter Gardens from the Grand Pier, September 2011. Rogers' Field had been suggested as a site for a summer and winter gardens back in 1881, but at that time development went ahead in the Boulevard (see page 64). The Town Advertising Association discussed how to develop this site again in 1914 but the outbreak of war brought other priorities and the field became allotments for food production. Finally, in 1922, the Urban District Council bought the field by compulsory purchase order. The Winter Gardens opened on 14 July 1927, giving the town a superb ballroom and entertainment venue. The ground between the pavilion and the High Street was turned into formal rose gardens, tennis courts and a putting green. On the left is Weston College, the town's tallest building. It opened in 1970 and has invited controversy ever since due partly to its height and size, and also because of its uncompromisingly modern style.

33

THE BEACH

BEACH STALLS, C.1902 (below). At this time there were some thirty stalls on the sands selling all manner of things from seafood to ice cream, soft drinks, buckets, spades and souvenirs. In the past, foreshore rights belonged to the lord of the manor whose agents generally allowed traders and entertainers to work unchecked. Eventually there grew to be so much happening

on the sands – donkeys, fairground rides, sideshows, concert parties, stalls, even wild beast shows – that some control was required. In the 1880s the town commissioners purchased the rights to the beach and brought in licensing. Trade was not allowed on Sundays and all stalls had to be removed every Saturday night to the respective owners' premises and returned on a Monday morning.

WESTON BEACH, SEPTEMBER 2011. Nowadays a few beach stalls continue to sell traditional seaside fare such as cockles and whelks, while others offer those holiday necessities like sun hats, beach balls and buckets and spades. Swing boats offer rides for young children and there are trampolines and go-carts further down the beach. Trading is also now permitted on Sundays and bank holidays.

BEACH LAWNS

BEACH LAWNS LOOKING south, *c.*1916 (below). Originally the whole of this area was wind-swept sand dunes. It was the influx of visitors brought by the railway from 1841 onwards that persuaded the town commissioners it should be improved. However, nothing further was done at that time. In 1883 the new Seafront Scheme was started for the construction of the three-mile sea wall and promenade. It also included landscaping the Beach Lawns with grass and shrubs. Later, in the 1920s, the rockery was built down the western side to provide a wind break. The first three houses on the left were demolished when the Grand Central Hotel was built in 1925. The Boy and Serpent

The Gardens from the B
Wes

cast-iron fountain was made by the Coalbrookdale Factory in Shropshire. It was donated to the town by Thomas Macfarlane in February 1913.

PRINCESS ROYAL SQUARE looking south, August 2011. The elaborate formal gardens with their corner gas lamps have been replaced by modern landscaping with additional seating in the newly pedestrianised space. The restored fountain is now the centrepiece of this area. In the distance is the Weston Wheel. In a poll in the local newspaper, townspeople voted to rename this Pier Square, but at the formal opening it was changed to honour Princess Anne who performed the ceremony in July 2011.

BEACH ROAD AND RICHMOND STREET

THE CORNER OF Beach Road and Richmond Street, 1938 (right). These properties were demolished soon after this picture was taken, with the intention of extending the Grand Central Hotel, which is on the left. Indeed the Promenade Hotel, next to Fortes Ice Cream Parlour is already empty and the window frames removed in this picture. The following year, however, the Second World War broke out and nothing further was done. It remained derelict for the next fifty or so years.

SEVEN CAFÉ BAR and Terrace, September 2011. This site had been empty since the Second World War and was not redeveloped until 2005. The building on the right of this

THE PROMENADE
PRIVATE·COMMERCIAL
HOTEL
BOARD RESIDENCE
BED & BREAKFAST

image was originally the Atlantic Cable Office. Several transatlantic undersea communication cables came ashore at Weston and this office relayed the messages to their destinations. During both world wars it was of such importance that the road was closed and permanently guarded, accessible only to those with a pass. The recent semi-pedestrianisation of the surrounding area has enhanced the setting considerably.

BEACH ROAD

BEACH ROAD, c.1910 (below). The large house to the left was on the corner of Carlton Street. Next to it is the tiny Camden Cottage. This was one of Weston's earliest holiday cottages. It survived into the 1980s before it was demolished together with its neighbours. The house to the left of the Grand Atlantic Hotel is Belvedere, built in 1811 for Isaac Jacobs, owner of one of the Bristol glassworks. It

was the first property built on what is now Beach Road. The Grand Atlantic Hotel was built in 1854 as The College, a private boys' school. It was converted into a hotel in 1889 and is still used as such today.

BEACH ROAD, SEPTEMBER 2011. The site today is occupied by Carlton Mansions, Weston's largest block of apartments. The new road layout at this now busy junction makes it hard to take a clear photograph of the current buildings. On the right is the base of the Weston Wheel, a popular smaller version of the London Eye, with great views over the town on a clear day. Behind the viewer was the Tourist Information Centre, which had been on that site since the 1920s, although a new building was opened there in 1973. In 2011 this was closed in Council cost-cutting measures and the services moved to part of the Winter Gardens pavilion. The site is to be redeveloped with a café and bar.

LOWER CHURCH ROAD

THE NATIONAL SCHOOL, *c.*1880 (right). This was on the corner of Knightstone Road and Lower Church Road. It was built in 1846 mainly at the expense of Bishop Law, a generous benefactor to Weston. The official opening of the school was postponed due to the illness and subsequent death of the bishop. There was accommodation for 160 boys and an equal number of girls, although by 1873 there were well over that number of regular pupils. Children paid twopence a week or a penny if more than one child in a family attended. In 1897 the boys' department moved to the newly-built Board School in Walliscote Road and for a time there were only girls here. On the extreme right you can glimpse the end of Oriel Terrace (built in 1847) and a walled plot. The School of Science and Art was not built until the 1890s. The National School, by then known as St John's, was demolished in 1966.

WESTON COLLEGE, AUGUST 2011. Weston Technical College was opened on 11 September 1970 by Viscount Amory as a tertiary vocational college. In 1998 it underwent a major facelift. The long flight of steps at the main entrance was removed and the entrance relocated at the side. The building was also painted and given new windows, both of which soften its previous stark exterior. The School of Science & Art next to Weston College in Lower Church Road used to house the Art & Design department of the college but this moved to the new university campus in Loxton Road, opened in 2007. The old building lay empty for a few years but in 2011 work began to convert it into multi-purpose teaching spaces and meeting rooms.

SOUTH PARADE

SOUTH PARADE, C.1869 (right). These elegant Regency villas were built in 1819. On the left is Myrtle Cottage, once home to Samuel Serle. Serle was an entrepreneur of astounding versatility. On a small watercolour portrait, painted in the 1850s, it lists his occupations as 'Parish Clerk, Sexton, Town Councillor, Beer and Cider seller, Brick & Tile maker, Public Library Keeper, Print Seller, Stationer and Toy Seller, Fisherman, Boatman, Hairdresser and Barber, Perfumier, Farmer, Grazier, Milkseller, Theatre Manager and Lender of Carriages and Chairs for Hire.' Myrtle Cottage was demolished in the 1870s and a bank built on the site. The Bath Hotel was also built in 1819 and was originally called The Masons Arms. In 1820 a regular four-horse coach operated from there to Bristol. In 1865, it was there that William Terriss, later to become a famous actor, stayed, when he was mistakenly thought by locals to be the Prince of Wales!

SOUTH PARADE, AUGUST 2011. Today the properties are all commercial. About 1870 the Bath Hotel was renamed The Imperial. Competition between The Imperial and Royal Hotel was always fierce as they are so close geographically and the story goes that, since the only person to outrank a king is an emperor, the name Imperial was chosen, to indicate its superiority over the Royal Hotel! In 2005, the redundant bank building became Barcode, a Youth Café funded by Weston Town Council with grants from the National Lottery. The Imperial is now a brasserie.

TOWN SQUARE

BUILDING THE EXTENSION to the general post office, Post Office Road, 1923 (above). The main post office, between Cecil Walker's shop and this new extension, opened in 1899 on what was originally the site of Verandah House. The buildings in the background on the right are those of the Royal Arcade. This ran behind the High Street from beside Cecil Walker's shop through to

Regent Street with a branch running at right angles to Salisbury Terrace. In the foreground is Rogers' Field, which belonged to the Royal Hotel before being bought by the local authority. It is seen here just before being cleared to build the Winter Gardens and pavilion.

THE SOVEREIGN CENTRE, 2011. In 1990 the post office, the remains of the Royal Arcade (most of it had been demolished in the 1930s), Trevors' shop in the High Street and the multi-storey car park behind Marks & Spencer were pulled down to develop the new Sovereign Shopping Centre. This undercover shopping mall offers retail units and a café with car parking for 850 vehicles above. It opened in 1992. While construction work took place, the formal rose gardens, tennis courts and putting green of the Winter Gardens were turned into a temporary car park. On completion they became the new Town Square, with seating, lawns and shrubs. The monthly farmers' market is also held there.

THE ITALIAN GARDENS

BUILDING THE ITALIAN Gardens, 1923 (right). Work began on developing Rogers' Field in 1923 with the first part – the formal Italian Gardens – completed a year later. This part of the scheme was separated from the Winter Gardens by a 61m long terrace of Portland Stone with statuary representing the four seasons. Probably brought from Italy, this was found for sale at Beddington House, Croydon. Henry Butt gave the purchase money and the partially-constructed garden was remodelled to make space for it. On the corner of Waterloo Street and High Street you can see Lance & Lance department store, Madame Windebank's millinery shop and Davies Brothers' stationers.

HIGH STREET, 2011. With the Portland stone terrace now in situ, it is impossible to reproduce this view exactly today, especially with the trees, planted in the 1980s, in full leaf. All of the buildings in Waterloo Street and the High Street were bombed in 1942. For many years after the Second World War this corner remained a derelict site, before being cleared for a temporary car park. Everything standing here today was built in the early 1960s, when the building line was set back further along Waterloo Street than before, creating a wide pavement area for shoppers on this busy corner.

THE HIGH STREET
(LOOKING NORTH)

HIGH STREET LOOKING north, 1905 (right). On the right the shops include Lance & Lance and Walker & Ling, both well-known local stores. Lance & Lance was Weston's largest department store until it was bombed during the Second World War and was never rebuilt. Walker & Ling are still going strong today, selling haberdashery, men and women's fashions, and drapery. In the distance is Grove Park and on the left, Rogers' Field – an open area of grass belonging to the Royal Hotel.

HIGH STREET LOOKING north, September 2011. All the premises on the left of the Gardens Restaurant were rebuilt in the late 1950s and early 1960s, following bomb damage during the Second World War. The street has been fully pedestrianised since the 1990s, a fact the café has taken advantage of by putting tables and chairs outside. Next to the café was Youngsters', an old-established toy shop. The building was Brown's Café before that. It was demolished in 1994 and the present shop built. On the left, instead of Rogers' Field as in the below image, are the Italian Gardens and Town Square, the latter replacing the formal rose gardens, sunken garden, putting green and tennis courts that existed there from 1925 to 1990.

MARKS & SPENCER

MARKS & SPENCER Penny Bazaar, 1908 (right). This was the year Marks & Spencer first opened a shop in Weston, at No. 57 High Street. In the 1820s this was the site of George Affleck's vegetable

shop. A tiny shed-like structure with earth floor, it was nicknamed the Gentlemen's Club as every morning the men of the village would gather there to gossip and exchange news. This shop, together with the neighbouring properties including the Plough Hotel, was demolished in 1935 in order to build a new modern and bigger Marks & Spencer store.

MARKS & SPENCER, September 2011. The 1935 shop was burnt out just seven years later when a nearby bakery was set alight by incendiary bombs and the fire spread. Marks & Spencer moved into temporary premises in Meadow Street, where it remained until 1954 when the present shop opened in High Street on their original site. The shop has been enlarged twice: once in 1972 when the demolition of the Plough Hotel in Regent Street provided room to expand and build a new food hall, and again when the Sovereign Shopping Centre opened in 1992.

THE HIGH STREET

HIGH STREET LOOKING north, 1970s (right). The High Street is one of the original roads of Village Weston. By the mid-nineteenth century it had developed into the main shopping street, as it remains today. The shops on the left include some well-known chains of the time such as John Collier and Keith Pople, both selling menswear, Salisbury's (who sold luggage and bags) and Marks & Spencer. On the right, next to the Midland Bank, is Maynards' sweetshop, Lipton's grocery and Stead and Simpsons' shoe shop. Traffic was still allowed access, although it was one-way southbound.

WESTON HIGH STREET looking north, September 2011. The buildings themselves have changed little, although nowadays there are many more service industries such as travel agencies, coffee shops and opticians rather than shops selling goods. The street is now closed to traffic and the central lamps with their attractive floral baskets add colour to the streetscape. The yellow table in the foreground belongs to Chaplaincy About Town or CHAT. They are a charity that has been set up by local Christians, to provide a listening ear to businesses, shoppers and anyone who frequents the Weston-super-Mare town centre.

THE PLOUGH HOTEL, REGENT STREET

THE PLOUGH HOTEL, Regent Street (below). This was an extension to the old Plough Hotel in the High Street, where part of Marks & Spencer now stands. It was to the Plough Hotel that

PC Robert Hill was taken in November 1847 after being stabbed by Tom Cann after a fracas at the corner of Regent Street and St James Street. Tom Cann was sentenced to seven years transportation to Australia. PC Hill survived and even went back to police work. However, he died in 1851 as a direct result of his wound. This is a superb example of an Edwardian pub, with tiled façade and etched glass windows. Inside was a huge mahogany bar.

MARKS & SPENCER, Regent Street, September 2011. Marks & Spencer had been looking to expand their Weston shop for some time and the acquisition of the site of the Plough Hotel was a good opportunity. The old hotel was demolished in 1972 after an auction to sell off the fixtures and fittings. In 2005 Regent Street was closed to all traffic other than taxis, buses and blue badge holders as part of a new traffic scheme around the Alexandra Parade area.

REGENT STREET

REGENT STREET WESLEYAN Chapel, *c.*1890 (right). The foundation stone for this building was laid in 1846 at a time when this part of the town was rapidly expanding. The railway had only been running to Weston for five years, leading to a huge influx at weekends and in the summer. Regent Street led directly from the railway station (then situated in Alexandra Parade), past the

end of the High Street to the seafront, the promenade having been extended south from Knightstone to Regent Street in 1829. The post office had opened in the 1820s in Clarence House in Regent Street, so this was a busy thoroughfare from the earliest days of the resort. The chapel underwent some rebuilding and the addition of this spire fourteen years later. When the chapel finally closed at the end of the nineteenth century it was converted to commercial use.

REGENT STREET, SEPTEMBER 2011. By 1903 the chapel had become a bank, which it remains to this day, and there are few outward signs of its previous religious foundation. Most of Weston's disused churches and chapels have been converted for new use, including the Wadham Street Baptist Chapel, now a community theatre, and St Saviour's church in Locking Road, now residential flats.

ST JAMES STREET

ST JAMES STREET looking north, *c.*1924
(right). This was the first part of the lower
town to be developed. Built in the 1840s,
one or two cottages from this period still exist
on the western side. It was a working-class
area, mainly residential, with cottages,
shops and workshops. There were two pubs:
the Globe and the White Lion Inn. In 1862
the Weston-super-Mare Co-op Industrial &
Provident Association was set up in Sydney
House. By the mid-nineteenth century the
street boasted some fourteen different traders,
among them a dairyman, beer retailer,
greengrocer, chemist, butcher, pork butcher,
stationer, watch maker, dealer in shells and
boot maker. The first fish and chip shop in

Weston (Coffin's or Baker's depending upon which of the two families you believe!) opened about 1900. Coffin's is seen here on the right. At the end of the road is the Plough Hotel in Regent Street (see page 56).

ST JAMES STREET looking north, September 2011. Sadly this road has declined dramatically. In 1960 the Co-op extended back from Union Street (now High Street South) into a vacant site created by the demolition of White Lion Cottages. Couch's owned three shops, and is probably remembered best as the stockist for local school uniforms. The 1970s saw the start of the decline, possibly hastened by the Dolphin Square development. Many properties are now empty; other properties are mostly restaurants rather than shops. Traffic is now one-way northbound from Oxford Street as far as Richmond Street.

GROVE PARK

SHELTER IN GROVE Park, *c*.1907 (below). Grove Park was once the grounds of Grove House, the summer residence of the Smyth-Pigott family, lords of the manor of Weston. The last lord of the manor, Cecil, sold the house and 8-acre site to the town council in 1889 for the creation of a public park, which opened on 20 June 1891. It was laid out with various features including, in the upper park, a rock-garden set in an old quarry with pools, waterfalls and rustic bridge and in the lower park, a bandstand and a large pool with a fountain. An 'old English café' was set up in

Grove Park,
Weston-Super-Mare.

the house and, in 1921, a memorial to the local people killed in the First World War was erected close by. In the photograph the shelter is lit, as is the fenced area, by gas jet lights encased in coloured glass shades.

SHELTER IN GROVE Park, September 2011. Grove House was hit by bombs twice during the Second World War and the ruins were demolished in 1952. The 1884 coach house can still be seen, together with a single-storey extension built about 1958. This is currently used by the town council as offices and mayor's parlour. In 2010 the shelter was converted into a café serving refreshments to visitors to the park. The park is once again used for a variety of events throughout the summer, including band concerts every Sunday and community music and dance festivals.

THE BOULEVARD

SUMMER AND WINTER Gardens, Boulevard, c.1920 (below). The idea of a winter garden for Weston-super-Mare dates back to at least 1881. In August that year the town commissioners discussed the idea of a place for people to go to enjoy the autumn and winter sun as the weather grew colder and 'a means of postponing the autumn and of mitigating the region of winter; a place affording shade, shelter, rest and recreation to some, while it will afford accommodation for fêtes, balls, concerts, lectures, croquet, lawn tennis and every description of out-of-doors amusements, not for summer or winter only, but for all year round.' The Summer and Winter

Gardens opened on 16 August 1882. The building underwent several changes of use, including a concert hall, roller-skating rink, cinema and theatre.

TIVOLI HOUSE FLATS, August 2011. The theatre was destroyed in the blitz of 1942. In June the Germans struck their heaviest blow on the resort when, on the nights of 28 and 29 June, two successive air raids took place. Over these nights 102 people were killed and over 400 injured when 97 high-explosive bombs and 10,000 incendiary bombs fell on the town. The site lay derelict for nearly fifty years. Finally it was developed in 1984 with this block of flats with offices and a retail unit on the street frontage. The retail unit has undergone several changes of use from estate agents to video rentals and is currently empty.

BOULEVARD BAZAAR

GRAY'S BOULEVARD BAZAAR, No. 20 The Boulevard, *c.*1906 (above). Gray's Fancy Goods Bazaar opened at the turn of the twentieth century. Prior to Mr Gray taking over, the shop was a grocery owned by Charles Harries. Mr Gray ran the bazaar until 1912, after which Mrs W. Gray was listed as the resident, joined a year later by a W. Govier. The shop window is fascinating and contains all sorts of things including dolls, baskets, toy ships, dolls' houses, model horses and even a toy donkey!

BENGAL RAJ RESTAURANT, Boulevard, August 2011. As in most towns, many retail shops have been converted to restaurants, cafés and other eating establishments, and also as everywhere, Indian restaurants are very popular. The first Indian restaurant in the UK opened in 1809, closing in 1833. The big resurgence in the popularity of Indian food came in the 1960s with the first Indian restaurant opening in Weston-super-Mare in the mid 1970s.

UPPER CHURCH ROAD

UPPER CHURCH ROAD, *c.*1906 (right). Although the road itself was built a little earlier, the first building work took place in Upper Church Road in the 1850s on the southern side. The northern side of the road was built in three stages, Park Row being the oldest, followed by Glentworth Terrace and then Park Crescent. By 1886 the road was more or less in its present form. These premises were all residential and it was not until the 1890s that they began to be converted into shops. The exception to this is the post office, which existed in 1886 but in premises next to what is now the Criterion public house. In 1909 you could buy pretty much all your everyday needs just in this one street as it boasted a chemist, fly proprietor,

boot maker, fishmonger and fruiterer, furniture dealer, two pubs (the Criterion and the Raglan Arms), grocer, baker, newsagent, dressmaker, greengrocer and refreshment rooms.

UPPER CHURCH ROAD, August 2011. Today most of the shops have changed back to residential use, although a few of the old shopfronts remain. The post office was a victim of the 2009 closures. There is still an off licence, two pubs and a general store. In 2000 builders were converting the shop nearest on the right into living accommodation and uncovered a striking old shop fascia board. In carved letters of black and gold it read 'J. Arkell, Pharmaceutical Chemist'. This dated to around 1911. In the earlier image, taken five years before Mr Arkell took occupancy, it is the building with the enormous gas lamp hanging over the door. The fascia has since been boarded over and is no longer visible, having suffered damage from vandalism.

THE DORVILLE

DORVILLE HOUSE, MADEIRA Road (below). Originally named Sutton House, this was built in the early 1850s. The first occupant was Samuel Baker, son of the founder of a local firm of solicitors

and Steward of the Manor of Weston. By the beginning of the twentieth century it belonged to Miss Baker, presumably Samuel's daughter. In 1914 Miss Baker died and Thomas Macfarlane, a local businessman and councillor, moved in with his family. Thomas died there in 1921. The next occupant was Leonard Guy, who was general manager of the Grand Pier. In 1933 the house was sold to Frederick Whiting, who, with his wife Dede, converted it into a hotel and renamed it Dorville House.

THE DORVILLE HOTEL, September 2011. The original house, which can just be traced from the two bay windows in the centre, was considerably enlarged in 1952. Joe Whiting, son of Frederick, took over the business in 1962 and ran it until it closed in September 2002. The building was sold to the Bristol Family Housing Association and for a short time was used as a hostel for the homeless. In July 2004 planning permission was granted to demolish the building and replace it with twenty-two flats. However, plans were then changed to a bigger scheme, planning to replace the building with forty homes, but this was refused and the building has remained empty ever since.

LA RETRAITE, SOUTH ROAD

LA RETRAITE ROMAN Catholic School for Girls, South Road, *c*.1970 (below). The building was erected in about 1859 as two large villas, Holywell and Woodlands. In 1881, Holywell was owned by Charles Girdlestone, a retired rector, or as the census so charmingly put it a 'Clergyman Without Care of Souls'. His sister Charlotte lived next door at Woodlands. Woodlands later became Forest Hill School and Holywell was opened as Coombe Ladies' College, run by Miss Astle. By 1910, the two houses were being run by Mr Ibbs as a boys' school. He retired that year and La Retraite Convent, who had opened a girls' school in Fortfield next door, was able to purchase Woodlands and Holywell. On the outbreak of the Second World War, the pupils of La Retraite were evacuated

to Herefordshire and this building was requisitioned as a Red Cross hospital. It remained as such until May 1946, after which it re-opened as La Retraite School. Two further houses in South Road, Pen Maria and Saltaire (renamed St Teresa's) were purchased as dormitories, adding Dunmarklyn in the 1960s, seen on the right, as pupil numbers grew. However, as R.C. Church Comprehensive Schools opened in the Bristol, the need for private Catholic schools was diminishing.

RAINHAM COURT, SOUTH Road, August 2011. La Retraite School closed in 1971, at a time when many private schools were struggling to attract sufficient pupils to survive. This was a period when Weston lost many of its largest and oldest buildings – Etonhurst, Villa Rosa and Kingsholme to name just a few – and La Retraite was no exception. It was demolished in 1986 after several years of lying derelict. Rainham Court was built on the site.

OVERCOMBE

No. 24 SHRUBBERY ROAD, May 2005 (right). Overcombe was designed by Robert Ebbels, a Wolverhampton architect better known for ecclesiastical architecture, and built in 1850 by John Perry. Perry was a partner of Samuel Harvey, a local builder and developer, but Overcombe was Perry's first independent contract. Built for Mrs Diana de Bruyn, it was designed in the Victorian Gothic style and built, unusually for Weston, of brick rather than the local limestone. The interior was grand with two carved white marble chimney-pieces (made in Lancaster) and a polished oak gothic-style staircase (made in Perry's workshops). The grounds were landscaped by Robert Adlam with lawns, shrubs and trees, one of which – a sweet chestnut – survives to this day. In the census of 1861 and 1871 the resident was Rachel Bennie, a gentlewoman and widow born in the West Indies. In 1881 the owner was Frances Townsend, a 41-year-old widow from Ireland living there with her mother, cousin Mildred

and daughters Henrietta, Elizabeth and Joanna, all looked after by a governess, housemaid and cook. In 1888 the house was enlarged with a new east wing designed by local architect Hans Price. Frances died in May 1891 and the house was sold to William Bennett. His children were born in Ceylon so he may have served with the East India Company or owned tea or rubber plantations. By the turn of the century the house changed hands again and at the time of the Second World War had been converted into four flats.

DESPITE A SPIRITED campaign by local residents, plans were approved in 2002 to demolish the house and replace it with flats. Uncertainties in the housing market meant it survived another five years but was bulldozed in June 2007. Overcombe House now occupies the plot.

THE RAILWAY

WESTON STATION IN the 1950s (below). This is the view that once greeted anyone standing on the railway bridge in Drove Road, near its junction with Locking Road. Weston was a busy railway station, with goods station, engine shed and three passenger platforms. To the left,

the track curves round into the main passenger station built on the loop line in 1884. A line of coal trucks is waiting on the siding behind the signal box, probably destined for the Gas Works. To the centre is the main goods station while round to the right are the excursion platforms. These were built in 1914 to take the long trains full of day trippers to prevent them blocking the main station.

VIEW FROM DROVE Road railway bridge, September 2011. The changes between this view and the one above are quite dramatic. Gone is the maze of tracks, signals and signal box. All that remains is a siding and the two lines into Weston station, hidden here behind Hildesheim road bridge. The signal box and coal trucks have been replaced by a car showroom, which highlights the change in transport from rail to road. Likewise, on the right, a coach and car park has replaced the excursion station and goods yard.

WESTON
CARNIVAL

WESTON CARNIVAL ENTRY,
14 November 1912 (right). This
won first prize for the most original
exhibit. It is pictured in Orchard Street
outside No. 42, the shop of Mr Gabriel,
undertaker and maker of window
blinds. The Weston Cycling Club began
the illuminated carnival processions
in 1889 with people in fancy dress on
bicycles and carrying lanterns. The
fire brigade was concerned about Guy
Fawkes Night and the indiscriminate
letting off of fireworks and so, inspired
by the cyclists, organised the first
November Illuminated Carnival in
1891. They continued annually
until 1914 when the First World War
intervened and following the war,
moved to becoming summer events.

WESTON WINTER CARNIVAL float, 2007. Carnivals restarted after the First World War in 1925, stopping again for the Second World War and starting again in the late 1960s when there were both summer and winter carnivals. The winter events are now part of the Somerset Guy Fawkes Carnival circuit that includes Bridgwater and six other towns. The Somerset Carnivals are regarded as the largest illuminated processions in the world, attracting crowds of up to 150,000 people. Dedicated Carnival Clubs fund-raise all year to build these spectacular floats, or carts, up to 30.5m long and 5m high. The largest have up to 30,000 light bulbs.

UPHILL STORES

UPHILL POST OFFICE and Café, *c*.1929 (right). Built on the corner of Old Church Road and New Church Road, it was run by Mr Coward, pictured outside the shop. Besides running the business, Mr Coward also published his own postcards of the village. Prior to this building being constructed, the Postal and Telegraph Office was next door in the end house of New Church Road.

UPHILL POST OFFICE and Stores, August 2011, is a sad sight and testament to the government's programme of post office closures in 2009, when not only Weston and Uphill suffered, but also Kewstoke.

A new use has not yet been found for the building and it remains shuttered. Meanwhile, Uphill Village Shop and Newsagent further along the road has been named Independent Community Retailer of the Year. Since the shop was taken over by new owners in 2006, it has been transformed into a thriving community-focused business. The store, open seventeen hours a day, delivers shopping to elderly and disabled residents free of charge and provides a home news delivery service up to a ten-mile radius, to help villages without a newsagent.

UPHILL WAY

UPHILL WAY, *c*.1910 (below). The original Dolphin pub burned down in 1860 but it was soon rebuilt, although the half-timbering is a later addition. The Ship Hotel further along the road has been serving the people of Uphill for over 250 years. Both pubs were used in the past by smugglers, who would guide French ships into the harbour by lantern light and swiftly unload and hide or distribute the cargo of brandy and silks. Uphill was a busy port in its day: cattle, slate and coal were brought in and bricks and tiles shipped out regularly. Between the two pubs is Ynisher Terrace, built in 1911. On the left is The Old Hall, with Mr Howe and his son Charles by the gate.

UPHILL WAY, AUGUST 2011. Not a great deal has changed. The Old Hall is now an Italian restaurant but the pubs remain popular and busy with residents and visitors alike. Uphill is a quiet village, protected by its geography from development and the huge housing estates that have since been built at Worle, Locking and St Georges. The building of the General Hospital at Uphill has been the largest new development in the area with the associated nurses' accommodation and increase in parking.

CORONATION ROAD, WORLE

CORONATION ROAD, WORLE, *c*.1905 (below). This road was named in 1902, the year Edward VII was crowned. The road is un-surfaced and there are no pavements. The house at the end of the road is West Acre, then the residence of Dr St John Kemm. His son Rupert was born there in February

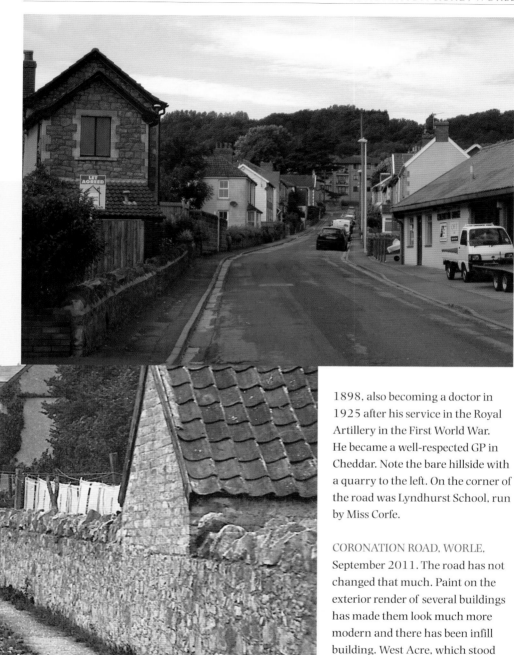

1898, also becoming a doctor in 1925 after his service in the Royal Artillery in the First World War. He became a well-respected GP in Cheddar. Note the bare hillside with a quarry to the left. On the corner of the road was Lyndhurst School, run by Miss Corfe.

CORONATION ROAD, WORLE, September 2011. The road has not changed that much. Paint on the exterior render of several buildings has made them look much more modern and there has been infill building. West Acre, which stood at the end of the road, has been demolished and Victoria Lodge flats built. Since the quarry ceased operations in 1970, shrubs and trees have softened the landscape.

LAWRENCE ROAD, WORLE

LAWRENCE ROAD, WORLE, is a tranquil rural scene of stone cottages and a fine elm tree in this photograph of *c.*1910 (above). In the centre on the picture is the Ebenezer Chapel, built in

1836 for the Nonconformists of the village. On the left, just out of view, is Myrtle Cottage, with the home of the village constable just behind that. A delivery boy can be spotted leaning on his bicycle on the left of the road.

LAWRENCE ROAD, WORLE, September 2011. This view can only really be recognised by the Ebenezer Chapel, now Worle Community Centre. The cottage on the right in the older picture can just be glimpsed behind the small tree and Lawrence Court flats. The elm tree was possibly a victim of Dutch elm disease, which felled so many trees in the area in the mid 1970s, or maybe it was cut down when the flats were built.

WORLE HIGH STREET

LOWER STREET, WORLE (right). This is Worle as it was: a rural village with un-surfaced roads and no pavements. Charles Bidwell recalled the village in about 1906: 'I well remember the white dusty roads. Candles and paraffin lamps were the only means of light in the cottages. All water was fetched from the village pump and we enjoyed the beautiful sight of horse-drawn carriages of holiday-makers from Bristol on their way to Weston-super-Mare.' The conical turret belongs to the laundry, a source of employment for many local women who could earn a shilling a day there in 1914.

WORLE HIGH STREET, September 2011. Most of the cottages along this road were demolished to make way for

the new shopping development of the early 1970s. Of those cottages that remain, all but one have been converted into shops. In the distance is the Woodspring pub, originally built as the New Inn in 1814. The road has been straightened and widened by demolishing the cottages and village pump that were opposite the New Inn.

THE SQUARE, WORLE

THE SQUARE, WORLE, *c.*1907 (below). Behind the photographer is the New Inn (now the Woodspring). This was a coaching inn, built in 1814, where extra horses could be harnessed

to coaches to make it up the steep Scaurs. When the foundations for the inn were being dug an ancient gilded bronze stirrup iron was found, indicating the road has probably been in use for centuries. Note the un-metalled surface with puddles of water. The tiny corner shop is Worle Coffee Rooms, run by Mr Pearne. Up the Scaurs, on the right, you can just glimpse some whitewashed cottages. These were almshouses for the poor of the village.

THE SQUARE, WORLE, September 2011. This is the busiest traffic junction in Worle today. The almshouses and cottages on the left of the photograph above were demolished in order to widen the road, and a new block of shops and a bank built in 1973. What was once a fairly narrow crossroads is now a large roundabout. This was all part of the planned expansion of Worle, which included the new housing estates north of the village.

THE SCAURS

GUNNING'S STORES, MAY 1973 (below). This was the oldest shop in the immediate area, the chimney bearing the date 1726. It was originally called Manchester House and this area at the top of The Scaurs was known as Manchester Square. From its earliest days the shop sold a wide variety of goods, from fabric to meat. Much of the produce would have been local. There was a

slaughterhouse at the rear and candles were made on the premises from the rendered pig fat or tallow. Dried goods and calicos would have been bought in. In 1826, Henry Rich established a Sunday school in the warehouse shown here on the right. To the right of the main entrance porch are steps to help people mount their horses.

SPINNERS COTTAGES, 2011. Gunning's Stores closed in 1985 and the complex, which at one time consisted of shop, granary, bakery, warehouse, slaughterhouse and butchery, was converted to residential use. The name Spinner came from a previous owner of the shop, J.W. Spinner, who took over the business from James Irish in 1895. The old shop windows and mounting steps still survive.

THE OLD FORGE, WORLE

THIS WAS ONE of two forges in Worle, the other being in Station Road (below). This part of Worle, together with the area at the top of The Scaurs and Church Road, is the oldest part of the village and is built on the dry higher ground. The road sweeping round to the right is very

old. It links Woodspring Priory, north of Kewstoke, to the medieval motte and bailey at Locking Head Farm. The road is very straight and both on Middle Hope and at Locking evidence of Roman occupation has been found which suggests it may be the line of a Roman road. The road down to the left is Hollow Lane, once an ancient trackway that linked the medieval fortified manor house at Castle Batch to the main village of Worle.

KEWSTOKE ROAD, SEPTEMBER 2011. The old forge and its associated cottage were demolished in 1973 to improve traffic flow and visibility. On the right is Springwell Cottage, which still has a well in the front garden. Prior to 1914 all Worle residents relied on local wells for drinking water. This had to be collected from various pumps around the village. There has been a great deal of house-building in this area at Pilgrims Way and along Kewstoke road over the intervening years, increasing the number of cars. It is now a busy junction used by traffic heading from Weston towards the shopping centre at Queensway and Priory School as well as to the new Court House at St Georges and onwards to the M5.

Other titles published by The History Press

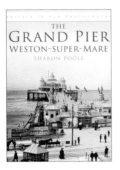

The Grand Pier at Weston-super-Mare

SHARON POOLE

For over a century, the Grand Pier at Weston has stood as a prominent symbol of this British seaside tradition. For over sixty years, the Grand Pier was owned and run by successive generations of one family, the Brenners. This book is also the story of how they constantly updated and improved the pier, ensuring its popularity with tourists continued into the twenty-first century. This book illustrates the history of this outstanding example of seaside piers, with memories and anecdotes from the people who owned it, worked on it, and loved it.

978 0 7524 4990 6

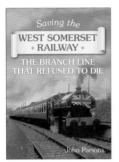

Saving the West Somerset Railway: The Branch Line that Refused to Die

JOHN PARSONS

The West Somerset Railway opened in 1862, linking Taunton, Watchet and Minehead. Popular with tourists travelling the Somerset coast, it was nonetheless closed by British Rail in 1971.This book tells the story of the small group of enthusiasts, many of whom still work on the railway today, who refused to let the line die. The railway was able to overcome its problems and become one of the leading heritage railways in the UK.

978 0 7524 6403 9

Haunted Somerset

JOHN GARLAND

This collection of stories and twice-told tales from around Somerset lifts the shrouds off many new and legendary hauntings, including some spine-tingling experiences as recounted to the author by Somerset townsfolk, villagers and visitors. Researching historical and contemporary sources, *Haunted Somerset* reveals its uniquely supernatural heritage including a coffin on the road, eerie Bath, the phantoms of Sedgemoor, Dunster Castle's ghostly sightings, headless horsemen, animal apparitions and Exmoor spectres.

978 0 7524 4335 5

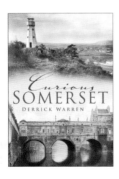

Curious Somerset

DERRICK WARREN

A great many curious and unusual buildings, objects and landscape features have survived the centuries here. This book is a guide to over 100 of these remarkable sights in a surprisingly undiscovered corner of the West Country. Over 150 old and new illustrations are included, together with a map and location details. *Curious Somerset* will make fascinating reading for residents and visitors alike, and will inspire many to explore this delightful county much more thoroughly.

978 0 7509 4057 3

Visit our website and discover thousands of other History Press books.

www.thehistorypress.co.uk